# GOD'S ONLY MISTAKE

MATTHEW SIMMONS

gaston
publishing
house

Published in the United States by
Gaston Publishing House

ISBN 978-0-578-82483-3

# DEDICATION

This book is dedicated to all those that seek freedom in their lives. My personal freedom journey began December 26, 2007 at Covenant Church Colleyville and it is my prayer that your journey to freedom in Christ begins with the reading of this book.

Your testimony will bare the name of the label you wore.

**National Suicide Prevention Lifeline**
**1-800-273-8255**

"This is such a powerful example of the power of believing and calling on the Lord for strength to get through the hard times to where you were called to be. A must read for everyone who has struggled, someone who has self doubt and lack of confidence which is all of us if we are honest. Learn the principles that could save your life."

*Dave Harms, Senior Vice President Primerica Financial Services*

"Matthew's Testimony is a refreshing short book good for anyone to read! In the beginning, he was open, honest and vulnerable about his past struggles and disappointments. Sometimes just knowing you weren't the only one feeling a certain way or went through a particular event is restorative in itself. Church hurts are real and so are self sabotage. The scripture references and biblical truths makes Matthew's Testimony a valuable work! I'm much anticipating what else Matthew has in store!"

*Rigel Mathis, Regional Vice President Primerica Financial Services*

"Matthew Simmons is one of the most God-fearing, kindhearted individuals I've ever had the honor of calling a friend. This book is a true testament of his story and molding him into the friend, son, cousin, brother that he is today. An absolute stand-up guy. After reading his story and his walk with Christ I believe he's an inspiration to many millennials who are dealing with their relationship with the Lord as well as the church. This testimony will truly help more lost individuals find their way."

*Danielle Reed, Regional Vice President Primerica Financial Services*

Matthew Simmons has opened his heart in a refreshingly honest and simple way that expresses the unconditional love of God for us all. All of us have doubts and fears and insecurities at times in our lives – even those of us that are "church kids". It can attack us at any age – even through people we know and love. Matthew tells his story of transformation to a victorious and happy and free life through his understanding, trust and acceptance of God's unconditional love. Matthew's story will encourage you. You will see how the power of God worked in Matthew's life, just as He can in your life. There are many life lessons for all of us in Matthew's story. You will be blessed by reading it.

*Richard Newton, Mayor, Colleyville Texas*

# TABLE OF CONTENTS

# FOREWORD

I have known Matthew Simmons since August of 2006, when Covenant Church merged with Matthew's previous church. When I first met him and his family, their love for God and people was evident. Matthew was intelligent based upon the conversations; he was skinny, extremely shy and socially awkward. I thought nothing of those things because he had a lot of light in his eyes. You could see that deep down inside he was a good kid who wanted what we all want and need...love and acceptance.

Matthew, no doubt was a church kid. Every time the

doors of the church were opened for services or some community event, Matthew was right there. He was zealous to please the leadership team and always had a "can-do" attitude. Slowly but surely, over the course of time, Matthew's transformation began to unfold right before our eyes.

Matthew graduated from a Home School Cooperative and attended Liberty University. Self-motivated and eager to learn, Matthew graduated from Liberty right on schedule. Now it was time to figure out what to do with his life. He and I along with about six or seven other guys began to meet regularly on Wednesday nights. It was in those gatherings where Matthew began to share his dreams and goals. He was challenged to stop talking about his future and to bring that future into reality. Matthew accepted the challenge, no matter how uncomfortable it made him.

This book is the result of the challenge accepted and I'm so proud of him. You will be inspired by his transparency regarding his struggles and how he overcame them. Matthew shares good thoughts about the word and the role it plays to get you moving in the right direction. In the end, like him, you'll have to take a deep introspective look into yourself in order to begin the journey of discovering who you are in Christ and what He's called you to do. Whatever that something is will require the assistance of others. Matthew's journey can certainly attest to the power of community providing encouragement and the 360 degree view to help identify blind spots in your life.

Congratulations Matthew for allowing the Lord to use you to encourage others who may have or currently experiencing the struggles you faced and overcame. I'm glad to be called your pastor and friend.

Ricky Texada, Senior Pastor, Covenant Church

# FOREWORD

# CHAPTER ONE

## WHY ME, LORD?

I'm not someone who had a troubled childhood. On the contrary, I grew up in church with loving, godly parents. I'm not a pastor's kid, but I am a church kid. My parents always had me in church with them. If the doors were open, we were there. At every church service, regional convention, local revival, and special event—we were there.

Yet, throughout my teen years, I multi-struggled with everything from social anxiety, depression, lust, and suicidal thoughts to church hurts, rejection, and feelings of inadequacy. As a boy, I was very quiet and shy. I walked on my toes, was homeschooled, and was very slim. A perfect recipe, I thought, for not being good enough. I overheard many times that I wasn't being raised right, that I wasn't eating enough, didn't talk enough, that walking on my toes would stunt my growth.

As I got older, the criticism changed to "Why do you still live at home; why aren't you dating; why are you doing that career; why aren't you going away to college; why don't you eat;why are you so skinny?" It seemed I was always being subjected to questioning. And oddly (and unfortunately) enough it always came from "church people."

The consistency of their questioning triggered feelings of distrust and disdain for anything that had to do with the church and its people. I felt like I was on the short end of the not-good-enough stick, and I was always being reminded of it.

In my teens, I was filled with insecurities about how skinny I was, which caused me to think the only way to be handsome was to have big muscles. In the church world, it seemed the only guys who had any worth were the ones going into full-time ministry.

In addition to the roller coaster of emotions that surrounded these insecurities, I also felt shame for even having these battles in my life. I grew up hearing Christians say things like "If you have enough faith, you won't have problems." But what does Scripture say about that?

Matthew 5:45 says that "God sends rain on the just and on the unjust."

So, we shouldn't be alarmed or surprised when a spiritual attack happens. We live in a fallen world that is full of sin, strife, and troubles. No one will leave unscathed.

During my teenage years, I chose to yield to these lies, to the idea that comparison was greater than compassion, that legalism was greater than righteousness, and that fear couldn't be replaced by peace. The sad thing was, I equated the way people in the church thought of me with how God thinks of me.

# WHY ME, LORD?

While it's true that God has a righteous standard,
it isn't true that He's in Heaven handing out
punishment, judgment, and disapproval
on His children. Unfortunately, many that
professed the name of Christ where judging and
disapproving. Thus began my insecurities. I saw the
world through the lens of my troubles instead of the
lens of reality.

The more insecurities I had, the more I started to think
that even God wouldn't bless me. I mean, why would
He? His own people kept finding fault with me, and
since He must behave like His people, then He has to
view me like they do—a mistake.

I did my best to shrug off these kinds of hurts, but
the wounds made a lasting, deep impact on me. For
example, anytime I would eat in public, I would imagine
that everyone in the place was judging my eating
habits and thinking badly of me.

These kinds of situations led to me developing a social
anxiety disorder at the age of 16. I felt that I couldn't
perform for people the way I was expected to, and

that I was under scrutiny from everyone around me. Unfortunately, I also thought I couldn't go to anyone in the church authority for help, because it would only fuel their attitudes against me.

I felt unlovable, and then guilty on top of that for feeling that way. I was still using the equation that a Christian who is having problems equals a Christian who has too much sin in their lives. Perhaps it even meant I was experiencing a lack of faith. I was full of doubt and wondering just how much sin I must have in my life for me to be having all these problems.

Of course, this is in no way biblical. Jesus says in John 16:33 that "In the world you will have tribulation, but be of good cheer because I have overcome the world."

Back then, I just couldn't see this passage pertaining to me. I was convinced that my lack of faith had caused my anxiety and depression. I was starting to believe subconsciously that the lie the devil had designed for my life—that I was God's only mistake—was true. In all of history, God said oops one

time, when He made me. Wow. What a label to wear
and a heavy burden to carry.

Satan knows how to use well-intentioned people
against you. That's why hurts caused by the church are
the worst hurts. Scripture refers to this in Zechariah
13:6, "If someone asks, 'What are these wounds on
your body?' They will answer, 'The wounds I was given
at the house of my friends.'"

No one should have to be on red alert
when they're in their own spiritual home. But that's
how I constantly felt as an adolescent in the church.
I never knew when the next not-good-enough
comment was going to come around.

My social anxiety disorder started manifesting itself as
severe panic attacks. These would be triggered when
I went out in public because I was afraid I would be
judged by total strangers or exposed to situations I
found threatening. I couldn't even leave the house
without experiencing anticipatory anxiety.

Living with anxiety and panic attacks is no easy task.

A panic attack can actually feel worse than a heart attack. First, it feels like the walls are closing in on you. Your skin gets cold and clammy and your stomach tightens up. Next comes the nausea, dry heaves, and vomiting.

Then the most frightening part.
Your breath gets shallow, which makes your heart rate increase. Finally, you feel your throat constrict to the point of choking. In fact, this choking feeling is the element within a panic attack that people fear the most.

I did my best to live with this kind of anxiety and these panic attacks; this was my world for the better part of two years during adolescence. I thank God I was homeschooled, because I don't think I could have made it through public school. And I thank God that my freedom was just up ahead.

# WHY ME, LORD?

# CHAPTER TWO

## BREAKING THE CHAINS

This toxic cycle of anxiety and panic attacks finally came to a head in the summer of 2007, while my family and I were on vacation in Branson, Missouri. For me, this vacation was pure misery. I was hundreds of miles away from my safe space and not at all familiar with my surroundings. Both of these things are particularly upsetting to anyone with extreme social anxiety.

I was constantly battling severe panic attacks during the trip. In fact, I was in such fear that I had to keep a book on natural remedies near me in the car at all times. In that book was one paragraph that basically said "the anxiety will pass after discomfort." For me, in that state of mind, that was all I had to cling to.

Sad isn't it? My entire hope came down to a paragraph because I couldn't, in my mind, trust God to be there for me. I couldn't possibly see Him loving me. And I just knew He was utterly displeased with me for even having this anxiety.

One evening during the vacation, my parents and I went to a show called the Dixie Stampede. The people who worked at the show were dressed in Civil War-era clothing, which made for a great photo op, so we stopped to take a picture with one of the girls who worked there. No big deal, right? Wrong. It was a very big deal for me.

This was my worst nightmare and my rock bottom moment. The girl was very pretty, and I was in the middle of a severe anxiety attack. My body ached with chills, my throat tightened, my stomach became queasy, and my hands clammed up.

As the progression of my anxiety symptoms took place, they had invited me to stand next to the girl for the picture. But I insisted on staying where I was. I knew that if I attempted to have my picture taken with her, it would bring on a full-blown panic attack, complete with choking and dry heaving. They eventually took the picture with me not moving, stiff as a statue. My parents and the girl looked at me with both shock and concern. That was the moment I realized I was in more trouble than I wanted to admit.

You can't be free until you realize you need to be, have to be free. I had finally reached a place where the pain of staying the same was more than the pain of changing the way I was. The change I needed to make was to turn to God. I needed to give Him the authority to deliver me from the pain and anguish I was living in.

I hadn't done it before, because I never believed that He had a desire to help me. I certainly knew He was capable of it. I never doubted His power. I just doubted His love for me. Not anyone else, just me. I had

## BREAKING THE CHAINS

listened to the lies of the enemy for so very long; lies that said I was unlovable, unredeemable, unworthy. I had carried the unbearable weight of feeling abandoned by God, hated by others, and being overlooked as insignificant.

When I finally sat down in my seat at the Dixie Stampede show, I was exhausted. Spiritually and emotionally, I was simply wiped out from carrying so many lies for such a long time. I couldn't hold myself up anymore, and under my breath, I cried out to God that if He would deliver me, I would give Him the glory.

Okay, so nothing magically happened. I didn't feel anything right away. In fact, for several months, nothing outwardly changed. Yet, something in me had changed. I was changing. I was finally giving God a chance to love me, something I had never done before.

In my limited understanding of the nature of God's love, I didn't comprehend that His love was truly unconditional. I felt there had to be conditions placed on it, because church people seemed to have conditions I could never meet. I wanted to be free from the shame of never feeling good enough. Now, I know what you may be thinking, "That's just how you feel. It wasn't really real." You're right. But what is true is that the fear of rejection is real even if the rejection isn't. Perception really is reality.

Several months passed after that fateful day in Branson. Then on Christmas Day of 2007 I was anxious the entire day. I had what is called a chronic panic attack; which basically means that you have this never ending anxiety and fear. It wasn't as intense as before, but it lasted longer. It felt like the anxiety was never going to go away. Not how anyone would want to spend Christmas.

I had already forgotten the vow I had made to God a few months prior. If we let it, pain will make us forget God quickly. I was consumed by my pain, anguish, and despair. Nothing seemed to be happening, and there was no end in sight.

The next day was Wednesday, and we had a church

service to attend. This night was no different than any other church night. Leaving the house was an effort. I was as anxious as I always was for church (or anywhere else for that matter). This particular Wednesday night, the youth joined the main service. During the service, the pastor made an altar call for anyone needing God to move in their lives.

God moved me this night—literally. It was like there was a spring in my seat that shot me up and catapulted me forward to the altar. I was one of the first ones to arrive at the front, and I immediately knelt down and gave my every struggle to God.

I could not hang on any longer trying to fix this myself. I knew that my nothing-is-really-wrong approach wasn't working. I rededicated my life to God and vowed never to walk in bondage of any kind again. I made the decision that I would do more than just believe in God, serve God, and know God. I made the decision to trust God. And that makes all the difference.

We can serve God and still doubt that He has our best

interests at heart. It doesn't mean we aren't saved. It just means we aren't showing up for the fight. Or that we're showing up to the fight already defeated in our hearts and minds.

The fact is, we are victorious in Christ. But the devil will always try to convince us that our past will not allow us to do great things for God. The devil will play mind games with us...if we allow him to. He will confine us to the sidelines of life... if we choose to let him.

Notice that each of us has to make the decision to yield to his lies. He only operates on invitation. Satan defeats by apathy and complacency. Every lie of the enemy will lead there, and fear will make us procrastinate acting upon our true destiny.

A few days later, I was feeling pretty good but not planning to go out anywhere. Even with lots of victories behind me, the knowledge of an outing still spooked me. As the day progressed, on a whim, my parents wanted to go to the mall, just to walk around and enjoy a day of window shopping. At first, I declined, claiming I wanted to watch football instead. Almost instantly, I heard the Spirit of God telling me to go to the mall. It took me aback, but I was obedient to His voice and went to the mall. Obedience gets God's attention.

I realize going to the mall doesn't sound like a major step for most people, but for me, the mall was one of the worst places for my anxiety. Being around a bunch of strangers, usually mostly girls who (in my mind) would all be judging me... no thanks.

But I walked into the mall and into perfect peace. I had no anxiety whatsoever! I felt like I was floating on a cloud. It was at this moment I realized two very important things. First, that I was free. Second, that God had required me to act on what He had done for me. Obedience gets God's attention, and with that attention comes the favor of Heaven.

I felt the favor of Heaven that day. Walking through the mall worry and anxiety-free, I felt my Jericho crumbling and my Goliath being defeated. I felt that God had come through for me for the first time. At that very moment, I felt the love of God and freedom in Christ—all while walking through a mall.

This is proof positive that God shows His favor and answers our prayers however He desires. His will is going to be done. As Jeremiah 29:11 says, "His plan is to prosper you, never to harm you."

When Satan attempts to throw those old foes back into my face now, I tell him that I walk in freedom and not in bondage. But even after that moment of freedom in the mall, I knew I still had areas in my life that needed surrendering to God before I could walk into the destiny He had designed for me. I was ready to have those rough edges sanded off.

# BREAKING THE CHAINS

# CHAPTER THREE

## SOCIETY IS CALLING

We can't fall prey to the pressure of attempting to get people to like us. This is something I myself have struggled with. Social media has made this a much more filtered world where comparison is king. I have been on social media for awhile now. I'm from the MySpace era. (Yes, that's right.) Tom was my best friend, and I remember the feature of top five friends. How I longed to be in that list with my friends. I would wonder sometimes why I was removed from the top five list or how long I'd stay there. My approval came from top five lists and social media acceptance.

## SOCIETY IS CALLING

If you haven't caught on by now, I am someone who
longs to be loved by others. During my teenage
years I was so consumed by the approval of others
that whenever I felt I didn't get it, I would fold
like a cheap tent. I placed the value I felt for my
own life upon the opinions of others, which is a
very dangerous thing to do. This lack of approval, or
perceived lack of approval, really fed my anxiety,
leading to hopelessness and despair. This turned out
to be a recipe for disaster and an invitation to the
unthinkable—suicidal thoughts.

I fantasized about dying. I was consumed by thoughts
of rejection. I believed I wasn't up to the standard of
what I saw on social media and that I didn't have it all
together even though everyone else did. I know how
ludicrous that statement is, because no one has it "all
together." I was so distracted with comparing myself
with others that I felt I had to be them in order to be
loved, appreciated, and respected by them. I would
look at the people around me, people on MySpace—
don't laugh—and see the airbrushed images of
them next to the tattered image of my life. It
just didn't compare.

This level of hopelessness is bad enough, but being raised in a church climate that said "enough faith and no problems" made my struggles even more compounded. I felt shame in wanting to die. I felt the shame of thinking God wouldn't set me free. I didn't see any other way out and I would lie in bed at night and my thoughts were captivated by fantasies of death, dreams in which I felt relief.

This all came to a crescendo one night in 2007. Deep down, I didn't want to die or take my life. I wanted to see if God would stop me and if I could clearly hear His voice. I got up off the couch to go to the kitchen to drive a steak knife through my heart. With every slow step, I hoped that God would stop me.

Halfway to the kitchen, the Lord snapped me out of it and I heard His voice clearly. He reminded me of all that I would be leaving behind, what I would be forfeiting if I followed through with my suicidal thoughts. As I stood there and thought about it with my logic, and not my emotions, I started to see a different picture emerging. My parents, church family, pastor, neighbors, even my dog all came to my mind. I thought about how they would all miss me and what my death would do to them.

I thought about my future—learning to drive, graduating high school, attending and graduating from college, getting my first job, my first place of my own, choosing a career, getting married. Once I really looked at the bigger picture of my life, I began to see that God actually had a plan for me. I had more going for me than I realized. I was more loved than I realized. That moment slowly turned my heart from a place of despair to a place of hope.

Anyone who can relate to my story, anyone who feels that the only way out is death, they need to know that there is hope. God does not weight you by the opinions of others. If He was able to rescue me from my despair, He is more than capable and willing to rescue anyone. I never thought that I could escape from my pain, but God came through for me, and I know that He can do it for all who despair. I felt that I had to measure up to the lives of others. But I had to see that my own life was worth living.

One thing I still have to remember is that someone
else's life and success should always be used
for motivation, never comparison. Comparison has
always been a struggle of mine, and it is certainly easy
to do that today in a society driven by the "perfect"
images we see on social media. As a communicator, I
see others who are much like me in age and experience
and they are, it seems, further along than me in some
areas. They have more followers, are more popular, and
have more opportunities. While my thoughts don't
drift to suicide anymore, they can still drift towards
discouragement.

What gets me through times of comparison and
changes is a scripture found in Jeremiah 29:11: "For I
know the thoughts that I think toward you, saith the
Lord, thoughts of peace and not of evil, to give you an
expected end."

I find hope in this scripture. No matter how low
I may feel about my life, about how it seemingly
doesn't compare to that of others, I know that God
is always working to bring about His great plan for
me. Our lives are valuable to God, and our steps are

ordered by Him. We don't have to add despair to a world already full of it. Hope is greater than despair; life is more precious than the temptation to end it.

# CHAPTER FOUR

## IDENTIFY TO CONQUER

As I was bogged down under the weight of the despair, I found one faithful companion—lust. Lust was my mistress, and pornography was her identity. I felt that if a woman wouldn't accept me then at least the image of a woman would.

My addiction to pornography wasn't just about lustful thoughts. I needed to know that a woman loved me. I needed a woman to soothe my self-image pains. I needed someone beautiful to tell me that she cared for me. Yet, I didn't have that.

## IDENTIFY TO CONQUER

I didn't know what it was like to have a woman say that I was handsome. I only knew what it was like to be judged and looked down upon. I wanted to live a romantic comedy, but instead I was living Mean Girls.

At that time, I felt that lust and pornography were the only way to have a relationship with a woman. My love language is words of affirmation, followed closely by physical touch. I'm the kind of guy who longs for the praise of others; I thrive on it. To not hear it from a woman (outside of my mom) destroyed my psyche. I was the not-good-enough kid. Too quiet, too shy, too slow, too... something. Not this, not that... you get the picture.

Even into adulthood it has been the same. Not enough money, not a nice enough apartment, not advanced enough in my career, not popular enough. But there's one big difference now. Now, I don't allow myself to be defined by the fickleness of people who don't know who they are or what they want.

This shift certainly didn't take place overnight, and

there is still room to grow for sure. But back then, I had finally come to the conclusion that if I wanted my life to look different and to be all that God has created me to be, then I had to make my own change. I couldn't expect anyone else to do it for me.

The first part of changing is recognizing that we have to change. This has been true through every personal story in human history. I mentioned earlier how I hit rock bottom and had that "eureka" moment concerning my anxiety. A similar moment helped me in this area of bondage.

One night in my loneliness, I asked God in a snarky way why I didn't have a girlfriend. To which God promptly replied that I did have a girlfriend. Lust was my girlfriend. Once I got rid of that we could discuss it again, but until then, God wasn't going to send His best when I was too busy settling for the devil's worst.

It was a hurtful revelation. But I saw no lies in that statement; it was true. I couldn't imagine living a life without some form of companionship, which was currently lust. If I couldn't have a girlfriend, at least lust and pornography could keep me company. That was my logic; not spiritually sound of course, but I still had chains on.

The thing about chains is that they make a lot of noise but no sense. I had a mindset that said I have to have someone or something that makes me happy. The problem? This is idolatry. I put marriage, a relationship, and the love of a woman at the center of my life and affections. That was where my focus was on instead of it being on God.

I couldn't fathom a life alone, because I didn't think God could fulfill me. I would even justify it by saying that I had physical needs to be met. He made me desire women, so that was what I was doing. Twisted, isn't it? Nowhere in Scripture are we to desire marriage or love from a person more than from God. Period.

A friend of mine, Ryan Leak, said it best: "Don't put God expectations on human connections." Yet, that is the very thing I did. I wanted a significant other to take care of my needs instead of Jesus. What pressure that is! Unfair pressure that no person is meant to carry.

A scripture that hit home for me during this time was Matthew 11:28-30: "Come to me, all you who are weary and burdened, and I will give you rest. Take my yoke upon you and learn from me, for I am gentle and humble in heart, and you will find rest for your souls. For my yoke is easy and my burden is light."

That last part—His yoke is easy. I had a heavy burden of wanting approval from people who wanted the same approval for themselves. Also notice, it doesn't say to cast all our burdens upon another person; it is not their responsibility to make us lighter. Yet, that was what I was saying to myself. I was going to find a woman and saddle her with the task of completing me and relieving me of all my pain. It's no wonder I couldn't find someone.

I wasn't all too willing, at first, to release this area of my life to God. But as time went on, the Lord started to show me that He wanted to be first in my life.

It could only be after that happened that a woman

who was also seeking after His heart first would come alongside me. I had to be a man of God so I could attract the same caliber of woman.

This made me take stock of who I was as a man. I had to take purity of mind more seriously, and I had to relinquish the thought that a woman could do God's job in my life. An opportunity presented itself in the spring of 2015 to attend a men's intensive event by Covenant Church named (at the time) Camp Freedom. A fitting name for sure as it would be an intense and life-changing weekend of spiritual growth for me. One that I will always be thankful for.

I made the decision that lust would not dominate my mind anymore. I vowed that I was a son of God, and I came to that realization at Camp Freedom. My love for God was deepened because I saw God as Abba Father.

I loved God as God but not as Abba Father. Up to this point, I had a very impersonal view of God. Keep in mind, I still thought God had made a mistake with me. This was the thought process I went into this event with. It was during this weekend, however, that I began to realize my view of God was seen through the judgmental lenses of professing Christians.

God saw me as a son. It was the self-righteous and judgmental people of the church who saw me as a mistake. Every shortcoming of mine would be amplified in their eyes. But God never saw me like that. God never let my shortcomings define me. For the first time, I saw God as a loving father.

That was the paradigm shift that needed to take place in my life. I couldn't be everything God created me to be until I came to the place where I realized God Himself wasn't against me.

I learned another very important lesson in that moment. I learned that I was behaving in a manner reflective of how I viewed myself. I didn't realize my self-worth as a child of God. I looked to a woman, not God, to validate my existence. I sought to seek the approval of others, not the love of God.

A son knows his place in the family and in his father's heart. I didn't know my worth in God's eyes. My worth was tied to the approval of others. I know I'm not the only person to feel that way. But regardless, it is a very lonely existence to constantly seek the approval of others.

My life changed when I came to know God as Abba Father, and He wants to have that same intimate relationship with everyone.

The verse that blessed me at that moment in my walk with God was Romans 8:15: "The Spirit you received does not make you slaves, so that you live in fear again; rather, the Spirit you received brought about your adoption to sonship. And by him we cry, 'Abba, Father.'"

I let the devil push the buttons of insecurity and fear in my life. If you are like me, then there are likely things that bother you constantly. The devil will always look for a way to push those buttons. For me, I saw the world through the lenses of rejection, insecurity, and fear. No matter what triggers our insecurities or doubts, God can change our perspective.

I still have to check myself when I start to feel a certain way. There are times when the old thoughts come back. How I personally combat those thoughts is through worship. Covenant worship is a go-to for me. Whenever I play the songs, I feel the atmosphere change. I take my eyes off of the problem and I put them on God.

When the devil wants to remind me how bad the world is around me, I look to the goodness of God. When the devil tries to convince me I will be rejected by others, I look to the love of God. I am a child of the most high, a son who was once a prodigal but has come home to a Heavenly Father who has arms wide open. His arms are wide open for you, as well.

# IDENTIFY TO CONQUER

# CHAPTER FIVE

## STEPS TO FREEDOM

I grew up in the self-righteous Bible Belt, where a lot of the time it was "come hear me preach but don't watch me live." I sure did grow up being preached at, but a daily walk with God was not often modeled for me to see. In fact, from the very beginning of my journey, I made a commitment to do the exact opposite of what I saw many preachers and communicators do. There should be no high horses in Christianity. Yet, I felt the glare from others on their high horses, and it made me hate Christians.

My life changed when I decided to serve Jesus Christ

and not the opinions of church culture. Jesus brings freedom; the Holy Spirit brings conviction. People, lost in their own righteousness, bring judgment and elitism.

I've learned that the first step in spiritual freedom is keeping Jesus at the center. This was the decision I made back in 2007 when I surrendered all my anxieties to God. I made Jesus the center; no one and nothing had the final say in my life anymore. There can be no freedom in serving the opinions of others. I finally realized that these criticisms never had roots in the love of Jesus.

It was people who made me feel like I was God's only mistake. It is Jesus who calls me son (Gal. 4:7). It was people who made me feel unlovable. It is Jesus who loves me (Gal. 2:20). It was people who overlooked me.

It is Jesus who always sees me (2 Chron. 1:9). It was people who criticized my every ambition. It is Jesus who has plans to prosper me (Jer. 29:11). It was people who told me what I couldn't do or what I couldn't accomplish. It is Jesus who says that I can do all things through His strength (Phil. 4:13).

When I put people and their approval at the center
of my life, I felt every sting of their shortcomings as
they pointed out mine. When Jesus became the center
of my life, I felt His unconditional love and peace.
Freedom in Christ does not mean being exempt from
the problems of the world. Instead, it is freedom
from the problems you are allowing to own you. That
is the hope I carry with me daily.

The moment my troubles in life didn't own
me anymore was the moment when I made
the decision to forgive. Step two in walking in
spiritual freedom is having a heart to forgive.
Forgiveness for those who hurt me didn't mean I
was condoning their actions.  Rather, I was releasing
their poisons from my life. I had to do this to heal.

I had so much animosity towards church people
and the women who criticized and rejected me.
I even had disdain for perfect strangers who the
devil had convinced me were judging me.

I had a deep-rooted bitterness towards the judging
congregants and many preachers I saw either on
tv or in person; and Lord knows there were plenty
of opportunities to be bitter. More than once,
I was picked on in school and accused of being
anorexic. Some people told me I didn't speak
enough while others told me I spoke too much. You
get the point. I had good reason to be bitter and
unforgiving, but bitterness isn't found in Christ.

Unforgiveness is incompatible with Jesus. To be truly
free, and to heal completely from the emotional
scars that I had—whether they were self-inflicted,
assumed, or actual—I had to release the pain I felt. This
meant walking in forgiveness. I forgave so I too could
be forgiven.

Jesus is very clear that forgiveness is the name of the
game. In Matthew 6:14-15, he said, "For if you forgive
other people when they sin against you, your Heavenly
Father will also forgive you. But if you do not forgive
others their sins, your Father will not forgive your
sins."

Forgiveness was at the root of my life-changing experience at Camp Freedom. It became the center of my experience. I had to forgive. I had to release the poison that was destroying me. I knew that part of the very anxiety I dealt with was due to the animosity I had toward others. My physical health was being literally affected due to the figurative poison of unforgiveness. I allowed people to live rent free in my head, and they never deserved it.

The scripture that defined my Camp Freedom experience was Mark 11:25. In this passage Jesus says, "And whenever you stand praying, forgive, if you have anything against anyone, so that your Father also who is in heaven may forgive you your trespasses."

I held a lot against a lot of people. It was tempting to only forgive the people whom I knew, but a question was asked of me that has forever changed my mindset. "How free do you want to be?" I heard that question constantly during that weekend at Camp Freedom. I had to really look at myself and ask that question to myself. Matthew, how free do you want to be?

## STEPS TO FREEDOM

The answer came to me. I had allowed people to keep
me from truly understanding the Father's heart, and
I wasn't willing to allow that to happen anymore.
Each moment of pain had only happened once. I was
the one who kept it playing over and over in my life.
I kept the moments of pain alive by not relinquishing
the anguish. I felt control and power over my pain
by embracing it.

Therefore, my freedom was inextricably tied to my
willingness to forgive. Was I unjustly judged? Sure, I
was. Did it hurt? Absolutely. Did me forgiving those
who wronged or hurt me justify and condone their
words or actions? No, it didn't. As these realizations
of forgiveness came to me, they lifted my burden; the
weight of their offenses came off my shoulders.
Don't miss this. If we miss this important moment of
faith, we will miss the freedom that Christ wants for
our lives.

I couldn't take any other steps to
healing until I forgave. At that moment, God knew
that I meant business. Anyone can amen and
hallelujah in the good times or at a church service.

But God knew what I thought towards people when I was alone with myself. I had to live my forgiveness in private, when it is just me and God. I could not put out my own venom in return.

Forgiveness is a constant process. I still to this day have to walk in forgiveness, because people can still hurt me. But I always remember, I have to forgive within my heart when these thoughts and insecurities flare up. Is this easy? Not always. Yet at the end of the day, I value my freedom more than I value my pride. Letting go of offense is the turning point in our walk with God. When this step is taken; the rest becomes easier.

# STEPS TO FREEDOM

# CHAPTER SIX

## WWJT

Freedom requires a change of mind. Wherever you see freedom of any kind, whether it be political, financial, or spiritual, you will always see a mindset change. The scriptures say that you can't pour new wine into old wine skins (Mark 2:22). When I took the step to be free, I had to change my mindset. I couldn't walk in a place of freedom with my previous mental shackles. My old way of looking at life was through the lenses of rejection, isolation, and bitterness.

Step three is to renew the mind. I had to renew my thoughts in Christ because if I didn't, I would go right back to my prior state of mind. The mind is powerful; it helps shape behavior. That's why the Bible puts so much emphasis on it. I had to change the way I thought, because that was where the root of my battle was found.

There was a toxic flow in my life. My negative thoughts became negative beliefs, which led to my negative attitude, and then culminated in my negative behavior. But I eventually learned that when my thoughts were fixed only upon my problems, I only found temporary solutions, not a cure for the deeper problem. I kept trying to put Band-Aids on wounds that needed greater attention. My lust, driven by pornography, was that Band-Aid. It was my automatic response to the rejection I felt and expected.

I expected it because the lens I was viewing life through made it appear everywhere. One thing about people is that we all have our ups and downs, our good days and bad days. But until I made the effort to renew my mind, I had never thought about it that way. I never gave people grace. I always assumed the worst, and that certainly isn't what Jesus would do.

I'm WWJD old. Remember those bracelets? The What Would Jesus Do bracelets were worn by seemingly everyone, including myself, as a reminder of how to treat people and how to act. However, I want to add a slight twist. WWJT—What Would Jesus Think.

That is the ultimate question, and Philippians 4:8 is the verse that defines what this looks like: "Finally brethren, whatever things are true, whatever things are noble, whatever things are just, whatever things are pure, whatever things are lovely, whatever things are of good report, if there is any virtue and if there is anything praiseworthy, meditate on these things."

That has become one of my life verses. The change of mindset that comes when that verse is applied is a night and day difference. Without a mind that is renewed, I look at everything and everyone as a slight against me. I expect to be rejected, snubbed, overlooked, and forgotten. When I apply that verse to my life through a position of prayer, worship, and fellowship with God, I extend grace to people, overlook an offense, and see myself the way God sees me—as a son and a king with a destiny.

Yeah, of course, there are still people who I have to remind myself also deserve grace. For all those who have worked or still work in sales, retail, or customer service, you'll understand where I'm coming from. I live in a part of the Dallas-Fort Worth area where some people like to remind others just how much better they believe they are.

I have to especially renew my mind in those situations. It's a daily process. I can't just read a verse when I feel like it and all is well. There have been moments when I have tried to get away with that. It never works.

I can't eat one meal a week and expect my physical body to be healthy and strong. The same applies to the spirit and mind. I can't just coast off of the knowledge I've gained in seminary, the ministry training sessions I've attended, or all the spiritual oversight and mentorship sessions I've had. I can't for one minute expect any of that to work unless I keep feeding my spiritual side daily with the Word of God.

No quick fix here. This is a spiritual battle going on. There is a constant fight for the soul and mind of mankind, and no one can go it alone. No one is that strong. (Believe me, I'll soon explain why going it alone will never work.)

My mindset kept me not only stuck in my thoughts, but it also made me stagnant spiritually—a dangerous place to be. I had also isolated myself from others—a really dangerous place to be. In the wild, a predator will always attack the isolated creature first. The weakest, youngest, and injured animal is the easiest prey for the predator. That is no different spiritually, as I have witnessed in my own life. My darkest moments have always come in isolation. Being around others does something to the psyche. We were not created to be alone. We see that in Genesis 2:18, and that applies to much more than just marriage.

The fourth step I needed to take was to be in a Godly community. I imagined a community where I would be uplifted, held accountable, supported, encouraged, and challenged. This is the DNA of freedom. How can I say that? Because the devil brings none of that. He doesn't want us to grow in any way, and he keeps us in spiritual bondage.

No one was allowed into the secret places of my life. I wanted to be in control of something, and I feared even more rejection. What would people think of me? What judgment would they have against me? How much more rejection would I experience if I was honest about my life? I imagine these questions have also crossed your mind. If not, you are a saint who needs a statue erected in your honor.

This is my personal definition of community, this is the definition I live by, and this is how I base friendships:

**Community is a place where you are safe to be vulnerable, allowed to be yourself without judgement, and are strengthened to use your gifts. Finally, community is a place where covenant relationships are forged.**

All of these are important, but I want to highlight that last part. Covenant is something that isn't done in this society. People can be fickle and self-centered. I have felt the sting of this throughout my life. People say they are there for you, but when you need them, they are nowhere to be found. Sound familiar?

But I have seen that covenant bond in the community I have in my life. A covenant bond is a three-in-the-morning phone call type of friend. People who are there for you no matter what. That is what community is all about. People who can speak into your life and can be there for you in the good and bad moments. The ugly moments and the mountain top moments.

I don't think I'm unique in my desire for people to love and value me. I certainly want that still, and that is not a bad desire. However, suppressing that desire for relationships is dangerous because it can lead to bitterness. I was at this place in life too. I saw how others had what I wanted, but I was too afraid,suspicious, and disheartened to pursue it too. The very friendships and community that I needed and wanted I was forsaking in my self-pity.

I see this so much today. As someone who is blessed with the opportunity to be a leader in ministry, specifically young adult ministry, I see young adults retreating to a place of seclusion and isolation. This action is based on insecurity and protecting themselves against more pain.

I can recognize this so well in others because I myself have been through the same battle for significance. No one wants to be insignificant, and no one wants to be overlooked. Just look at the plethora of social media and dating apps which prove my point. The outrage about racism, sexism, elitism and classism is also an indicator of how people want to be treated as equal.

What I have had to learn in my life, due to this culture that seeks approval but not commitment, is that the only one that can truly provide what I'm looking for is Jesus Christ. He is the only source of unconditional love and he will never leave me or throw me away (Deut. 31:6).

The love of God sees redemption and is the greatest expression of grace. My life changed when I began to extend grace to others. In my life, I had to give people the chance to accept me. I had never thought about it like that. I was amazed at how many people actually wanted a friendship with me once I stopped being cynically guarded. I had always presumed rejection from everyone I encountered. When I finally began to extend grace to others, I also realized that they had many of the same insecurities as myself.

My fear, anxiety, and mistrust of people began to melt away when I realized how many people felt the same way I did. I was amazed that I wasn't alone. The devil had convinced me that I was by myself in my feelings and that God made a mistake with me—two devastating lies I held to be truth.

Two things occurred once I stopped believing these lies. The first is that I found friendship. I've been blessed to spend the majority of my 20's in a community with incredible young adults who value a strong faith in God, lasting friendships, and a good life together. I am blessed to know so many amazing people, and we do have a lot of fun together. I consider myself a wealthy man because of the friend circles I'm blessed to be in.

I believe that our truest wealth is always connected to the number of people who our lives impact for good. It also comes from how many people have impacted our lives for good in return. I can say that I have been impacted and loved by so many amazing people. Many of whom are reading this book, and to all of them I thank them for making my life an adventure.

I am blessed to lead a group of young adults who embody community. I have felt the love and acceptance that comes from that community of people. I have had my good days and bad days. My good moments and my bad moments. Through it all,they have been there. Not only for me but for each other, and that is a beautiful thing to be a part of.

I have experienced the safety of community. And as a leader I seek to create that environment for others. I have learned to create and be an active part in the environment I seek to be a part of myself. I seek to foster community as a leader. This type of community and friendship doesn't come casually.

I have never seen fulfillment come without a price. I haven't come to a place of friendship and community with so many amazing people by isolating myself from others. Community takes commitment.

This is where I have seen many people drop off. This

is the scariest part for many because transparency is necessary. The hallmark of any great community is safety. If, for whatever reason, you don't feel that you are in an environment where it is safe to be transparent, then I suggest you keep moving on until you find a group of people who are there for you no matter what.

Once this is in place, you will experience what I love the most about community—covenant relationships. This is what sets community apart from fickle friendships that the "swipe right or left" culture has cultivated. A covenant relationship doesn't look for a way out. A covenant relationship is a blood brother type of relationship. One forged in a deeper commitment to each other.

This culture of covenant relationships is continually being fostered in me at my home church here in Dallas, Covenant Church. (Yes, the name of the church is intentional.) At Covenant, we work to intentionally know God, find freedom, discover our purpose, and make a difference.

This is not just a mission statement; it is a culture and a way of life. That is what covenant relationships are. I'm passionate about this because my life has changed so much for the better because of it. Through covenant relationships, I've grown spiritually, been challenged to grow, and have had opportunities to prosper.

This book is a result of covenant relationships from people who want to use their gifts along with mine in an effort to get this story into your hands. The biggest benefit for me in my covenant relationships is that I have been encouraged to think differently about myself. The men and women in my life today won't settle for my old way of thinking.

This leads to the second thing to occur for me when I stopped believing the lies of the devil. I discovered a new way of thinking. I'm loved. I'm cherished. I'm a masterpiece. I'm valuable. I'm worth knowing. I'm a friend. I'm worth hiring. I'm handsome. I'm productive... You get the picture.

Everything that I never thought about myself is

exactly what I believe now. I know who I am in Christ, and I have people in my life who want to see God's plan for me come to fruition.

I pray that you have people in your life who encourage you to think and believe this way. I pray you have these important friendships that will better your future. Remember, iron sharpens iron (Prov. 27:17).

If these relationships are not present in your life, I encourage you to seek out those people who look to give and not take, people who will be there for you in the uncomfortable and difficult times of your life. It doesn't take much to be there in the good times, but it takes a commitment to being in covenant in the tough times.

I have seen all of these steps work in my life, and they still work today. I am a better man now, having walked each of these steps in my life. I am not this way because of the goodness of Matthew Simmons and my ability to transform my own life. Rather, my transformation is completely due to the saving power of Jesus Christ.

**WWJT**

# CHAPTER SEVEN

## GOD'S MASTERPIECE

Jesus Christ has the power like no other to transform lives and deliver troubled souls. In our own strength we cannot save ourselves, and we cannot positively think our way to a better life. The scriptures are clear about the heart of mankind apart from God.

As it is written in Romans 3:10-12, "There is no one righteous, not even one; there is no one who understands; there is no one who seeks God. All have turned away, they have together become worthless; there is no one who does good, not even one."

# GOD'S MASTERPIECE

The depravity of mankind is certainly not a popular opinion in a humanistic world, but my life wasn't transformed by being good enough for people around me. It has been transformed by the matchless love of Jesus Christ. Jesus will never give up on us. He certainly hasn't given up on me. In a "cancel culture" where everyone is giving up on people at the first sign of offense, Jesus is not canceling anyone.

The Gospel of Jesus Christ is simple, and it's found in John 3:16. "For God so loved the world that He gave His one and only Son, that whoever believes in Him shall not perish but have eternal life."

A relationship with Jesus Christ is the ultimate covenant relationship. I would be remiss if I didn't extend an offer for you to know the Jesus I know personally. Many people know of Jesus, but there is no intimacy and fulfillment in knowing of someone.

There are many people I know of, but if I walked up to them, they would have no idea who I was. Don't let that be said about our relationship with God. I'm including myself in that statement because I certainly don't want to hear as in Matthew 7:23, "depart from me I never knew you."

The love of Christ is available to everyone. Jesus didn't pick and choose which sins to die for, and he didn't die for perfect people. Jesus' free unmerited favor—the gift of salvation—is open for all, no matter what we have done or what our background is.

Jesus hasn't let me down—and he won't. He has been with me every step of the way, even when I didn't think he would want to be with me. Scripture says in Deuteronomy 31:6, "Be strong and courageous. Do not be afraid or terrified because of them, for the Lord your God goes with you; he will never leave you or forsake you."

It is my prayer that you come to find the same saving love and grace that I have found. God thinks you are worth dying for. Do you think that He is worth living for? His love is matchless, His sacrifice is priceless, and living for Him will leave you victorious.

I once believed that I was God's only mistake.

## GOD'S MASTERPIECE

Today, I know that I am a masterpiece fearfully and wonderfully made (Jer. 1:5). The love of God and redeeming work of Jesus has truly transformed my life from a mistake to a masterpiece. My prayer is that you will allow God to do the same for you.

# EPILOGUE

How does a parent express in words what is in their heart for their child?  When Matthew was born, my life and world gloriously changed.  From the moment he was placed in my arms, I was overwhelmed with a joy unspeakable, and filled with awe that my Heavenly Father entrusted and  blessed Dean and I with his life to train him up in the nurture and admonition of the Lord.

I began to see things differently, through my Heavenly Father's eyes, and the responsibility placed on us.

## EPILOGUE

As I watched Matthew grow, I saw how the Lord was preparing him for the call on his life. Saved at a young age and baptized in the Holy Spirit, he was preaching around the house as a little boy. As he grew, it was apparent Satan also saw God's call on his life. Being a former teacher, I knew the public school system well and we agreed that I would retire and teach our son. We began home schooling, and as Matthew has shared, many disagreed with our decision and let us know. Unfortunately, children hear those people. As a parent, you want to protect and fight for your child, and you do to a certain extent, but there comes a time as your child gets older, that they need to fight their own battles, as Matthew has shared.

To see him struggling, and walking out his faith, was heart breaking. As a parent who loves their child, I reaffirmed Jesus' love for him and let him know He is always with him. I took him to the promises in God's Word, loving him through this journey, and interceding to the Father for him. The Wednesday night he went down for prayer, I was rejoicing as my prayers had been answered. Seeing how the Lord had delivered and set him free, brought such joy. To watch his hunger for the things of God grow was glorious.

Matthew has been through much, but Satan never had a chance, because as a child of the Most High, you are never a mistake! Matthew has become a man of integrity and honor, representing the Kingdom as an ambassador, and I could not be more proud. He is focused on his race, and will not be uprooted, which has a lot to do with his name.
When we knew we were having a boy, God gave the perfect name: Matthew Jacob. Both are strong names: Matthew, meaning gift of God, which he is, and Jacob, meaning supplanted: one who holds onto.

To say that I am proud of him and what he has accomplished in this book by sharing his testimony... there are not enough words.

When he graduated from High School, I wrote a poem to him which still holds true today and I would like to share it.

*So you think it's over, well that's that,*
*The answer to this thinking is no.*

## EPILOGUE

*It's the beginning of your destiny and dreams,*

*Your Father in Heaven says so.*

*You've been trained in His Word, excellence, and honor,*

*His integrity dwells in you.*

*Take what you've learned to advance His Kingdom,*

*As He directs what He's called you to do.*

*You are somebody in the Kingdom of God,*

*And will do great and mighty things.*

*So rest is Him, His presence, and Word,*

*As He gives you new songs to sing.*

*You're a fine young man-anointed and blessed,*

*As people have said to me.*

*I agree with them all, what more can I say,*

*The Lord has blessed me with you, you see.*

*By Tina Simmons*

A wise man will hear, and will increase learning; and a man of understanding shall attain unto wise counsel; Proverb 1:5 KJV

Something I say all the time to him: you are the head and not the tail; above and not beneath; blessed going out and coming in; strong and courageous; an anointed mighty ambassador of the Kingdom!

# ACKNOWLEDGEMENTS

There are so many to thank for this book coming to fruition! I am thankful for my Lord and savior Jesus Christ for His work in my life. Without Him and His delivering work in my life I would not be the man I am today. I am very grateful and thankful for my parents Dean and Tina and for their work not only on this book, but for how they raised me. I want to thank my team of editors Debbie Sharp, Dean Simmons and Jeannette Smith for there work in editing and formatting this book! Thank you to Reggie Sharper for the about the author photo. Thank you to Christopher Newton for helping with the first wave of promotional

# ACKNOWLEDGEMENTS

material. Many thanks to my publisher, Gaston Publishing House, for making this book a reality! Jeremy and Kasey Gaston both made this possible along with the entire Gaston Publishing House team! I want to thank everyone that wrote a review that is published in this book and for my pastor, Ricky Texada, for his foreword, as well as his spiritual leadership in my life.

Thank you to everyone on my launch team who has helped promote the book on social media, and for all those of you who have prayed for this book. I thank you. Your prayers have been felt and seen, and this book would not be possible without them.

Matthew Simmons is an author, public speaker, podcaster, and entrepreneur. His passion is what he calls Stylish Leadership, which is a wholistic approach to leadership that looks at Faith, Family (relationships), Finances, and, Fashion. He often shares this passion by speaking at schools, churches and on social media platforms about financial literacy, men's fashion, and faith-based topics. His podcast Stylish Leadership can be heard on: Anchor, Google Podcasts, Spotify, Breaker, PocketCasts, RadioPublic, and Stitcher.

## ABOUT THE AUTHOR

Matthew is on the board of directors for the School of Entrepreneurship for MacArthur High School Irving TX, and assists in the coordination of young adult small groups at his home church, Covenant Church Colleyville. He resides in the Dallas/Fort Worth metroplex and is a graduate of Liberty University with a bachelor's in Religion.

CPSIA information can be obtained
at www.ICGtesting.com
Printed in the USA
LVHW010443220221
679515LV00005B/1235